Tree Frogs

Nature's Singing Chorus!

Love of Nature Series

ISSUE 22

Dr. Richard A. NeSmith

dr.nesmith@gmail.com

http://richardnesmith.obior.cc

Dr. Richard A. NeSmith
Winter Haven, FL 33884

DEC 2020

ISBN: 9798569883660

FLESCH-KINCAID GRADE LEVEL: 7.5

Tree Frogs

The term *tree frog* is a **common name,** and common names can create misconceptions. Such is the case here, as well. For example, not all tree frogs live in trees, bushes, or hedges. Not all frogs found in trees are *true* tree frogs. Some tree frogs do live in trees, whereas some live on the ground, and others live underground. However, we can look beyond this inconvenience. We will recognize the term in light of the scientific classification of those within this group of **amphibians**.

Tree frogs, also treefrogs, are amphibians of the order **Anura** and include over 4,000 species worldwide.[1] Tree frogs tend to be small, have slender legs, and have slit-like horizontal pupils. Those frogs that do live in trees are called *arboreal,* which explicitly refers to trees.

---

[1] Tree frogs from the order Anura, and the family Hylidae are the most numerous. Anura is divided into three suborders.

Range

Tree frogs are found on every continent but Antarctica. They are most diverse in the tropics of the western hemisphere. Of the **4000 species**, 507 species live inside of the Amazon forest. There are seven genera of tree frogs

with 30 species in North America. Though the Southwestern deserts are not ideal habitat for some creatures, many frogs, tree frogs, and toads are found there. Most have unique adaptations to help them survive the warm and dry environment.

INTRODUCTION TO AMPHIBIANS

The word **amphibian** comes from two Greek stems, *amphi,* and *bios.* Amphi- means *both,* while –bios means *life,* from which we get the word *biology.* The branch of science that studies amphibians (and reptiles) is called

herpetology. Those doing so are called **herpetologists.**[2]

The idea is that amphibians live *both* in water and on land. These animals live a *double life.*

All amphibians share these **characteristics**:

① cold-blooded (*ectothermic*)

② moist, scaleless skin

③ can breathe through the skin

④ tetrapods (four feet)

⑤ require water or *damp environment* for egg-laying.

Some tree frogs are aquatic, and some are terrestrial. Some are semi-aquatic. However, they share many characteristics in common.

---

[2] *herpein* means "to creep."

Characteristics

There is no specific name to distinguish a male frog from a female. A group of frogs, however, is called a ***chorus***. Tree frogs can come in lots of sizes, usually regulated by species. Most arboreal species are small to tiny because leaves and small branches hold little weight. Sizes can vary from 4-5.5 inches (10-14 cm) long to as small as 1.5 to 5 inches (3.8-12.7 cm).

North American tree frogs are commonly called **gray tree frogs** in the United States.[3] Some of our tree frogs are dull green, with the insides of their thighs being bright yellow. Colors vary greatly within the same species. Coloration tends to provide camouflage benefits, enabling them to hide from predators or act as a warning.

---

[3] Europeans tend to call them *North American tree frogs* to distinguish them from the European variety.

Amphibians are cold-blooded vertebrates, in a class making up frogs, toads, newts, and salamanders. They all have an *aquatic* **gill-breathing** larval stage, typically followed by a terrestrial lung-breathing adult stage. Amphibia (pl.) usually live on land but breed in or over water.

Since nearly all tree frogs are from the order **Anura**, let's take a closer look at them as a group. The term Anura means *without a tail*, so these frogs' tail-bone **(pubis-ischium)**[4] does not extend out past its body. They generally have long, powerful hind legs that fold underneath their body, shorter forelimbs, webbed toes (without a claw), and then, of course, no tail extending beyond the body.

They have large eyes and special glands to moisten their skin (making it slimy). Though there are toads in the order

---

[4] Made of calcified cartilage.

Anura, tree frogs have *smooth skin* compared to the toads' warty skin (though there are some exceptions).

Canyon Creek tree frog.

Because a frog's skin is so vital to its survival, we must consider this **organ**. The skin is porous and easily absorbs water and chemicals through **diffusion**[5] and **osmosis**. Water passes freely and is the primary way that a tree frog stays hydrated. Water can also diffuse out, causing dehydration.

Apart from protecting a frog from harmful bacteria and

---

[5] Diffusion is the net movement of anything from a region of higher concentration to a region of lower concentration. For example, inside of a frog the concentration of some chemicals, such as sodium and chlorine, is greater than the concentration outside. This causes water to enter (**osmosis**) their bodies in order to dilute the concentrations until they are equal. For more information look up *hypertonic*, *isotonic*, and *hypotonic*. Just as a frog will have to monitor thermoregulation, it must also monitor hydration versus dehydration.

The resonating vocal pouch acting to amplify sound.

fungi, the *primary* function of the tree frog's skin is to regulate body moisture. Not only is water needed for egg-laying, but it must be available for a frog to **hydrate**. Rarely does a tree frog drink water, but may do so from water droplets on plants or condensation. Instead, frogs *absorb water* from the habitat's surrounding moisture through their skin.

Under most circumstances, a tree frog will locate a small pool, even if just captured by a leaf, and sit in it for a time.

If this water is accessible, then the frog may do this several times a day. The mucus secretion on the skin is absorbent, but also, the skin on the frog's inner yellowish thighs of the hindlegs is even more porous. Once rehydrated, the frog will move on.

The mucus absorbs water and is highly resistant to **evaporation** because of a waxy covering from a wax gland. This helps the frog to maintain much of the water absorbed. If overly exposed, the mucus will dry out, and the frog will then lose moisture and eventually die. Under extreme conditions, some frogs will form several layers of mucus on the skin. Some species who burrow themselves for months (or years) require this for survival (and is more common among desert-dwelling species).

Tree frogs do not swim. Though their skin can absorb oxygen from the water, they have lungs and can easily

A frog egg cluster.

drown if these become filled with water. Some tree frogs living in any of the five U.S. rain forests[6] may not ever have to concern themselves searching for water until breeding season.

One of the main characteristics of real tree frogs is the *sticky pads* on their toes.[7] It appears that both mucus and suction-like properties assist in climbing and holding fast. These pads are so efficient they can climb on the side of wet glass, vertically on a wall, and recently it has been found they can walk upside down on ceilings. Some have additional skeletal structures in their toes.

---

[6] See: https://www.traveltrivia.com/rainforests-in-the-us/XqgZkXU1XQAGkiDo

[7] Scientists learned in 2007 that the angle of the toe pads and a secretion of mucus were involved in the frogs' ability to stick to wet, smooth leaves, rough, dry trees and other surfaces. See: https://bit.ly/36RdSVO

Arboreal tree frogs are generally walkers and climbers. Climbing is aided by the expanded toe tips with sticky adhesive pads. They do not, however, tend to be jumpers.

The presence
of cartilage
between the
last two bones
of each toe
enhances the
ability to
climb. This
feature allows
the tips of the

toes to swivel backward and sideways, with the pad remaining flat against the surface. Those in this order who make their homes on the ground lack the toe pad feature and are, instead, active leapers.

Tree frogs can be of various colors, but most of the species found in the United States are green, gray, or brown. Again, common names cause some confusion, for a "green" tree frog may not appear green at times. Tree frogs change colors in reaction to their environment and their activities. Sometimes the upper body can be spotty, resembling lichens with brown or grayish coloration. Patterns can vary.

Tree frogs also seem to have unique features when it comes to their skeleton. Many of the normal bones are significantly reduced in size and number from the bones being fused together.

Most frogs see well only at a distance but have excellent vision at night. Their eyes are especially sensitive to movement. Peripheral vision helps tree frogs to spot predators and prey. They can see color even in the darkest of the night when a human could see nothing at all.

They have two transparent eyelids, one on the bottom and one on the top. A third semi-transparent eyelid, called the ***nictitating membrane***, protects the eye underwater and keeps it moist while on land. Humans focus the eye by changing the shape of the lens. However, treefrogs focus by moving the lens back and forth within the eye, focusing

much like a camera or binoculars.

Frogs can hear but do not have ears like us. They have eardrums and an inner ear. The frog's ear is called a **tympanum** and is the circle behind the frog's eye. The ***tympanic membrane*** picks up sound waves. The *vibration* *spot* near the lungs quivers and shakes in response to sound and possibly a means of identifying sound direction.

Frogs can hear sounds up to 38 kilohertz. This is the highest frequency any amphibian species have been known to hear. In comparison, humans can hear up to about 20

kHz and typically talk at 2 or 3 kHz. However, the frogs' range of hearing is limited. Their ears are sensitive only to the frequencies of sounds they need to recognize.

Habitat

Whether it is in swamps, mountains, or deserts, *moisture* is the key to survival, and water is the key to reproduction. Tree frogs live in wetlands (swamps and marshes), pastures and grasslands, forests, brushy territories, and arid environments. Some have even done well in urban and suburban neighborhoods and have been found to breed in swimming pools. Those tree frogs in the wild breed in shallow lakes, sluggish streams, occasional pools, livestock watering tanks, side-of-the-road ditches, and water-filled tire ruts. **Breeding** sites are used for short periods during the **breeding season**, lasting from weeks to a few months. Breeding season usually aligns with the rainy season, which

is also when food is most available. Tree frogs then spend the rest of the year in higher ground homes.

It isn't uncommon to find tree frogs a few hundred yards from water. During dry periods and in arid areas, adult tree frogs are active only during the night while spending the day in water or shaded vegetation, under rocks, in log cracks or animal burrows, or other protected places.

Reproduction

All frogs reproduce **sexually**, meaning there is always a male and a female. The female will lay the eggs (**spawn**) in still water. At the same time, the male simultaneously releases **sperm** in the water to fertilize the eggs. All frogs lay eggs in water, and fertilization is *external*.[8] To make sure that the sperm lines up with and reaches the eggs, the male and female get into a mating position called **amplexus**. The male climbs onto the female's back and hooks his

---

[8] There are a few exceptions here as a few species of frog use internal fertilization. In this case, the eggs are fertilized inside the female's body before they are released.

forelegs around her middle. Frogs can remain in amplexus for hours or even days.

The female releases as few as one or as many as several hundred eggs. Inside, the female has provided each egg with a yolk sac as a food source until hatching. Not all eggs hatch submerged or with parental care.[9]

A **tadpole** is the *larva* form of a frog. It has a rounded-sickle-shaped body with a long tail, small fins, and external

---

[9] A general rule of thumb is that the larger the number of eggs laid the less parental care provided. Some tree frogs that lay only a few eggs will stay around and monitor the offspring, ensure water availability (even urinating in their flower-pool) or lay unfertilized eggs for them dine on.

gills (functioning like a fish's gills), removing oxygen and exchanging carbon dioxide. The process begins and produces a very different looking larval form than that of the adult. This change is called **metamorphosis**.

Though these "steps" vary with species, the eggs are laid in clusters or **egg masses**. The eggs are contained and held together in a gelatinous egg casing, which expands as it absorbs water. It acts to protect the eggs as well as to ensure adequate moisture.

Frogs can *spawn* one or two eggs. Others can spawn up to 4,000 eggs at one time. Some eggs are laid in plants that hold small amounts of water. Other eggs are laid on the tips of leaves of plants growing over water, ponds, lakes, ditches, or slow-moving streams. Those eggs laid on leaves will, upon hatching, drop into the water, where they will fall into the water source below and begin to grow as a

Invasive baby Cuban tree frog on a naked lady bloom.

tadpole. A few frogs lay eggs directly into the water. Frog eggs are highly sought after by snakes and other animals and are full of protein. The tadpoles' survival rate up to metamorphosis was very low (about 0.8%; that is 8 out of 1000).[10]

Depending on species, most frog eggs hatch within one to four weeks.[11] Tadpoles tend to be brownish and vary

---

[10] Survival rates in specific locations are always dependent on the actually number of predators present. Some unborn tadpoles can sense the vibration from a predator and can move causing premature hatching so that some escape and have a chance to survive.

[11] Some hatch as quickly as 36-48 hours, but seems to be related to environmental conditions demanding rapid growth and development in order to survive.

greatly in size, both during their development and between species, and differ between 1.3 inches (3.3 cm) to 4.2 inches (10.6 cm). Non-fertile eggs do not hatch.[12] Frogs can breed between two and three years old. They often return to the location where they were spawned, and males attract females by croaking. In this species, females lay their spawn in well-vegetated, shaded, shallow ponds.

As the eggs mature, the spawn clusters/egg masses (also called **clutches**) swell and float to the water's surface. Frogs lay from one to two clutches of eggs per year. If a frog lays two or more clutches per season, generally, it will lay fewer eggs than laid the first time. The developmental period between a frogspawn being laid, growing as a

Pacific Tree Frog

---

[12] die by *apoptosis* (programmed cell death that occurs in multicellular organisms) if they are not fertilized

tadpole, and young frogs leaving the water is about 14-16 weeks.[13] The odds of survival at this point for the next 12 months improves to approximately 10-25%.

An adult frog has lost its tail, the gills have been reabsorbed, and the lungs become enlarged. Breathing enables the frog to leave its watery home and live on land. It is during this transition that the adult frog begins to change its diet and food sources.

Just behind the eye one can see the frog's tympanum, which is a thin membrane for hearing.

Male tree frogs are much smaller than females (**sexually dimorphic**). For some, there are also color differences. For others, it is more challenging to determine the male from female.

The males croak to attract females, and other frogs croak or chirp out warnings to those they view as romantic intruders. Almost all male frogs attract mates with nightly **mating calls** and announcements. The musical call, usually after dusk, can last four hours. Frogs have vocal cords, just like humans. They also have a **vocal sac**, which works as an *inflatable amplifier* (resonator).[14] To start calling, a frog breathes in and then closes its nostrils. Male tree frogs use the call to form a **breeding territory** and to find a mate. Chirping announces the male frog's fitness. The *loudest*

---

[13] Some frog species can remain in the tadpole stage as long as two years and be rather large before reaching adulthood.

[14] Amplification is done by the cheek or throat pouches.

male frog gets the mate. The female will search for him and fight off or avoid all others. All in all, it gets pretty noisy.

Tree frogs also have *non-mating* calls, including a territorial clucking sound and a high-pitched distress call. That will

physically fight off rival tree frogs and defend their territory, and some calls are warnings to others. Victors often also win the local female.

Faster chirping frogs tend to be heftier and in better physical condition, assumedly because it requires energy to chirp. To chirp faster, a frog has to take in more oxygen and consume more energy.

Singing, croaking, and calling can fill the summer air. Though most breeding occurs by early June, gray tree frogs sing throughout the summer, especially on chilly, wet nights. Hearing one of these is quite impressive because it is a big sound coming from such a small creature.

Diet

As **tadpoles** (newly hatched frog eggs), they become full

time eating machines. They begin as filter feeders and **herbivores,** eating algae and nibbling on plant stems, leaves, and any dead insects they encounter. The larger they grow, their mouth forms like a rasp in which they can cut and gnaw on plants and dead animals. A growth hormone controls its growth. This hormone develops progressively in higher and higher doses as they grow, *speeding up* even more growth and development exponentially.

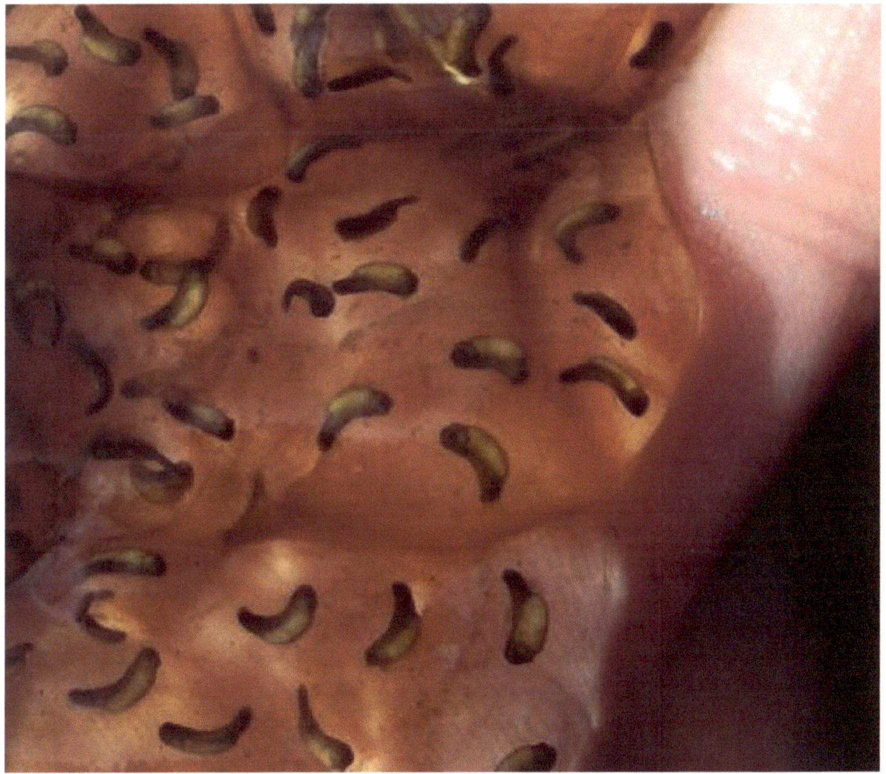

Egg cluster with growing pre-hatched tadpoles.

They begin eating on anything they can find or catch, including *scavenging* dead animals. Larger tadpoles will catch and eat live insects. Forearms and hindlegs develop inside the skin and eventually are pushed out, much like putting one's arms through a shirt or blouse.

In the final stage, the older tadpole changes so that the raspy mouth becomes a hard beak. Even more voracious in their appetite, tadpoles become fierce and aggressive **carnivores**, but to the degree of becoming **cannibalistic**. They begin consuming the lesser fortunate and lesser

developed tadpoles. Eating other tadpoles is believed to *speed up* growth even more. They are now getting additional

Gray Tree Frog

growth hormones from the victim tadpoles they consume. As metamorphosis continues to change their bodies, the tail is reabsorbed. The stomach, which initially digested plants, is now changed to digest animal protein. The jawbone begins to take a new shape, widening to the mouth we recognize on frogs.

One of the unique situations here is that the offspring never compete with their parents. Tadpoles and parents not only live in different environments but eat different types of food.

As adults, all tree frogs are **carnivores**, but more specifically, they more precisely are **insectivores**. Most tree frogs are **nocturnal** and hunt in the understory of wooded areas in trees and shrubs. A specialized tongue is attached at the front of the mouth. The frog flicks it out with great accuracy. The tongue (called a **spit**) is rather long as it is about one-third of its body (less than one inch long at the most). This is quite huge in size comparison. The spit is full of sticky frog saliva but has adhesive forces up to 1.4 times

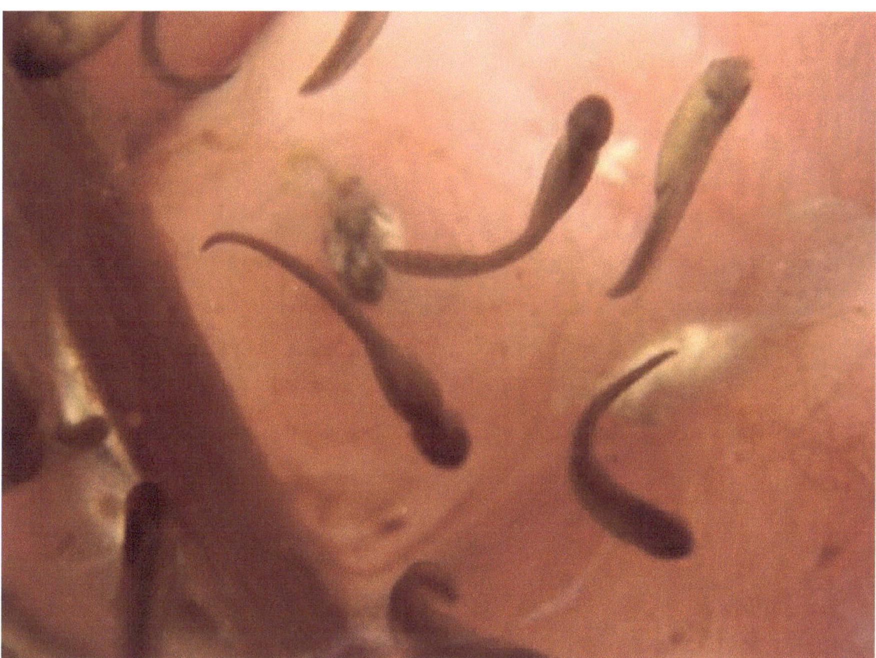

Maturing tadpoles

the body weight. The sticky tongue could lift nearly twice the frog's body weight.

Arizona Tree Frog

They search and eat living flies, ants, crickets, and beetles. They will also consume snails, dragonflies, mosquitoes, grasshoppers, moths, earthworms, nightcrawlers, and other small invertebrates. Larger frogs will pursue larger prey, including mice, snakes, birds, little turtles, fish, and other frogs.

Adult frogs can survive for an extended period (3-4 weeks) without eating, but survival will require eating about the equivalent of 10-12 full-grown crickets a few times per week.

Behavior

Ectotherms utilize **behavioral mechanisms** as a means to control their body temperatures. Monitoring temperature, body heat, and hydration is a constant need.

Benefits of being Cold-blooded

Amphibians, like reptiles, are **cold-blooded** animals. This term means their liver does not produce all the heat necessary from metabolism for life as it does in mammals. This state is called **poikilothermic** because their internal temperature varies considerably. Another similar term used is **ectothermic**, meaning *outside heat*, referring to where they will obtain that needed body heat.

Metabolism includes all the processes whereby an animal consumes food that is broken down into smaller molecules.

Besides using components of that food, it also provides nourishment for cell growth, repair, and energy production (in the form of ATP[15]).

Enzymes, made of proteins, regulate an animal's metabolism. Enzymes, however, work within specific ranges, including pH and *temperature*. To not have to produce most of their own body heat means they require less food. The main benefit of being an **ectotherm** is that no energy is wasted trying to gain this body heat. The heat needed is collected indirectly from the environment (primarily from the sun). The benefit of this type of metabolism means less food is required to sustain life.

Disadvantages of being Cold-blooded
The average length is between 6 to 21 days after fertilization. Tadpoles: consist of gills, a mouth and a tail.

---

[15] ATP = adinosine triphosphate

The disadvantage of being an **ectotherm** is that survival

dramatically depends on self-regulation.[16] This requirement is not quite as delicate for reptiles, for at least they have a dryer, more waterproofed skin. But it is more pronounced for amphibians. A cold temperature slows down the metabolism, which also then restricts muscle movement. They have to monitor both *temperature* and body *hydration* to ensure that they do not dry out or overheat.

One clear means of regulating body temperature is moving out of the sunlight or moving to shelter in a cooler and more protected location. Terrestrial frogs may dig a burrow or bury themselves in the litter. Green tree frogs hide under tree bark or inside a tree hollow to cool down. Just like for turtle and alligators, this is an ongoing task.[17]

If a frog becomes too hot, it may retreat to water, even if it is just water captured in a flower or orchid. Water is cooler than the air and so cools the frog through **conduction** but also **rehydrates** it. This process is called **evaporative cooling** and stabilizes its body temperature. When the heat

---

[16] Called thermoregulation.

[17] See the *Love of Nature* series, Issues 3 (*American Alligators & Crocodiles*) and 11 (*Freshwater Turtles*).

is high, water **evaporates** from the skin of frogs, producing a *cooling effect*. Losing water, in this case, ensures a proper body temperature. Wetness and moisture are vital for a frog's survival and another reason why frogs are restricted

Ornate Tree Frog

to environments with adequate water sources nearby.

Besides moving into, out of, or near water sources to control temperature, tree frogs can also change **color**. Color assist in the *regulating* of body temperature. Their bodies changing color affects how much solar radiation (heat from the sun) is received, absorbed, and evaporation occurs through their skin. Darker colored frogs tend to warm up more quickly, and lighter colored frogs cool off more rapidly. When temperatures are cooler, frogs then need to bask in the sunshine to warm up enough to be able to move.

In addition to behavioral mechanisms needed for a frog to regulate body temperature, coloration is also used as a **defense mechanism** to ensure safety through **camouflage**. Camouflage, also called **cryptic coloration**, is a tactic that organisms use to disguise their appearance, usually to blend in with their surroundings. Organisms use camouflage to mask their location, identity, and movement. Many frog species can change their color and pattern. Gray tree frogs (Hyla *versicolor*) are known to go from green to

Late-stage tadpole with tail yet reabsorbed.

gray or brown in seconds. Barking tree frogs (Hyla *gratiosa*) change their colors and display dark spots or unicolored skin to help camouflage.

Finally, some tree frog species need to survive seasonal cold, hot, or arid conditions. As a result, they undergo what is called **aestivation**.[18] Aestivation is a physiological/

---

[18] This is prolonged torpor or dormancy of an animal during a hot or dry period. Comes from Latin: *aestas*, summer, but also spelled estivation in American English.

chemical state. Here the body functions all slow down to a dormant state, even to the point of making it difficult even to observe vital signs.

Key characteristics of aestivation include:

❶ overriding the body's normal metabolic rates[19]

❷ retaining body water

❸ saving (conserving) energy and body fuel reserves

❹ altered nitrogen metabolism (controlling urine produced buildup)

❺ mechanisms preserving and stabilizing organs and cells

❻ mechanism preserving and stabilizing macromolecules over many weeks or months of dormancy.

The results of such biochemical changes include heartbeat and breathing slowing with some diffusion through the skin occurring. Body temperature dropping to nearly match the environmental temperature and the extended passing of time in a state of dormancy.

These are vital needs in times of prolonged drought or heat or both. In such periods the frogs *sleep* in a shelter (or underground) for months at a time. While aestivation occurs, some frogs produce a mucus cocoon or retain their shed skin covering to prevent water loss.

Desert frogs are often inactive or underground for the duration of the highest times for desert heat. Sensing the coming of rainstorms either by feeling the vibration from thunderstorms or sensing the moisture change from seepage will become active again. Shortly after such a desert

---

[19] metabolic rate suppression

storm, the desert becomes a chorus of frogs.

Frogs also repeat the same process to escape the freezing temperatures of winter. Upon spring, things revert to a normal state. Frogs emerge from hiding and may even appear to dig out of the mud or return from deep holes or crevices in trees or logs. Some will emerge from where they burrowed down under the leaf litter.

Sampling of Eight North American Tree Frogs:

	Name	Unique Characteristics
	Arizona Tree Frog Hyla *wrightorum*	• Dorsal bright green, with a dark, lateral line on each side that may be broken into several segments • posterior surfaces of the groin and thighs are orange or gold with a greenish tint • call of male frogs is a series of short, low-pitched notes, sometimes produced as distinct, metallic clacks or given as a trill • tadpoles are brown dorsally with minute silvery-gold flecks • skin of H. wrightorum is toxic and can severely irritate the eyes of humans after handling
	Barking Tree Frog Hyla *gratiosa*	• large treefrog, with some adults approaching 3 inches in total length • bright green to brownish with scattered golden spots and flecks on the back and a broad, irregular yellowish or whitish band on each side of the body • can live in treeless environments • may call during rainy periods from mid-May through mid-July. • breeding season cry is a hollow-sounding "donk" or "doonk" given at intervals of one to several seconds. • can also make a barking dog sound.

	Cope's Gray Tree Frog Hyla *chrysoscelis*	• very similar to the Eastern Gray Tree Frog (Hyla versicolor) though tends to be smaller and is more often green than its lookalike relative • warty skin and prominent adhesive pads on fingers and toes. • color varies from green to light greenish gray, gray, brown, or dark brown. • a few large, irregular dark blotches are usually present on the back; white spot on belly. • large white spot is always present below each eye. • a high-pitched buzzing trill.
	Eastern Gray Tree Frog Hyla *versicolor*	• color changes in response to its environment and activities, and can range from green to gray or brown. • blotchy pattern that resembles lichen • just over 2 inches long as adults • granular (almost warty) moist skin • Call sounds like a musical birdlike trill
	Green Tree Frog Hyla *dryophytes*	• medium-sized, and up to 6 cm (2.5 in) long • usually green in shades ranging from bright yellowish-olive to lime green; but colors can change based on lighting and temperature • sometimes skin has small patches of gold or white may occur • white, pale yellow, or cream-colored lines running from their jaws or upper lips to their groins • abdomens are pale yellow to white • calls frequent in between March and September
	Ornate Chorus Frog Pseudacris *ornata*	• 25–38 mm (1–1.5 in) in length • color varies by location: green, others red or brown with pure white belly • yellow spots in front of the hind legs • lives among longleaf pine flatwoods • nocturnal and are rarely seen, except during mating season • repeated rasping trill of most chorus frogs, sounding more like an insect
	Pacific Tree Frog Pseudacris *regilla*	• low 'krrreck' sound • juvenile frogs smaller than a dime • green or brownish with a black mask from the tip of nose to shoulder • secrete a waxy substance that keeps its skin moist • voracious predators, not picky eaters • eats its own skin when it sheds

	Pin Barrens Tree Frog Hyla *andersonii*	<ul><li>vibrant green and boldly marked</li><li>purple stripe with yellowish-white border</li><li>from the tip of now through the eye</li><li>down each side of the body</li><li>orange patch beneath each hind leg that shows upon jumping</li><li>purplish tinge under throat, especially in males</li><li>call is rapid, frequently repeated nasal quonk-quonk-quonk,</li><li>requires specialized acidic habitats so right at home in the pine environment</li></ul>

Miscellaneous

Many different carnivorous animals consume tree frogs. Mammals, reptiles, birds, and fish all eat tree frogs. Arboreal species avoid ground-dwelling predators by hiding in trees. Camouflage, along with bright colors and skin toxins, do often help frogs survive natural predators. The average lifespan of tree frogs in the wild varies between species. Some tree frogs can live up to 15 years, while others live for only 5-9. Some of the smaller tree frogs live for only 1-3 years.

The main threat, however, to frogs in North America tends to be more human-related. In general, frogs have become recognized as indicator species due to their *sensitivity* and responses to toxins, poisons, and various chemicals. *Frogs are the first to be affected when an ecosystem begins to degrade.* Their dwindling numbers may be a warning to us that our planet is *becoming* unlivable and unsustainable. No matter what's behind the decline, the disappearance of frogs is cause for concern.

Currently, a few of the serious issues focuses on **three**

main concerns:

❶ *being overcome and destroyed by Chytrid fungus.*

This fungus is also known as Bd.[20] It is a mysterious pathogen that kills amphibians by disrupting the delicate moisture balance maintained by their skin. It stops their skin from regulating water and electrolytes' movement. It has wiped out over 200 species and so far has no cure. By the time a frog shows symptoms, it dies.

❷ *having developmental abnormalities and extra limbs forming due to human pharmaceuticals.*

Nearly every medication humans took eventually leaves their kidneys and flushed down as urine into *sewers* and *septic tanks* or *water treatment plants*.[21] Also, farm animals now receive a lot of various drugs, from antibiotics to growth hormones. These all enter the water system, sometimes after treatment, and ultimately reach watersheds and aquifers. As a result, so do various medications flushed out by the body. These eventually come in contact with tree frog eggs and tadpoles.

As a result, pharmaceutical and hormonal contaminants, including bisphenol-A, antibiotics, and opiates, are being detected in a significant portion of the United States'

---

[20] Batrachochytrium *dendrobatidis*

[21] See **Pharmaceuticals in Water**. USGS. Available at: https://www.usgs.gov/special-topic/water-science-school/science/pharmaceuticals-water?qt-science_center_objects=0#qt-science_center_objects

groundwater supply for drinking water. It is unknown what amount of these chemicals will make it through water treatment back to the tap. Measurable amounts are being found in some rivers, streams, and other water sources.

In some areas, frogs are exposed to birth control medication from eggs to hatchlings and right up through metamorphosis. Male frogs exposed to low doses of **estrogen** have been found with egg sacs next to their testes, and where other male frogs would attach in amplexus and fertilize these male-laid eggs.[22] This is a rarity and not natural for any species of frogs.

Deformities are also just the tip of the iceberg. The effects of opiates and other narcotics are not even known. Scientists share that they have no idea what to do and may only be in the observation stage, that is, to watch and see

---

[22] Birth control pills (BCPs) contain human-made forms of two hormones called **estrogen** and **progestin**. These hormones are made naturally in a woman's ovaries. BCPs can contain both of these hormones, or have progestin only.

what happens. However, that is a terrifying and possibly costly ecological expense. What we find may not be reversible.

❸ *continual loss of habitat.*

As more forests are cleared and more woodlands stripped for neighborhoods, shopping centers, roads, highways, thoroughfares, and even farming operations, we know that we will affect many tree frogs' ecosystem. Land frogs, and toads, likewise, will be affected. Fewer habitats will be available, and the breeding grounds, in particular, are susceptible, under stress, highly sought, and pivotal for survival.

Eastern Gray Tree Frog

The greatest fear is that **we just do not know** what these changes will do to the frog population. We know that frogs are a vital component of the ecosystem and play a central role in many ecosystems. Tree frogs are an essential part of the food web, both as predators and prey. Remove the frog, and the entire system becomes unstable. They control the insect population and are a food source for many larger

animals. Frogs seem to provide an ecological balance. We may not be able to reverse the situation if we do not begin to protect them now from these threats.

In some communities, scientists are beginning to capture various frog species and place them in **"ark"** refuges to preserve them. In some cases, they are trying to produce through breeding and genetic manipulation a **gene pool** that will be immune, for example, to the devastating fungus. Some promising results are being made in successfully returning some of the ark frogs to their old habitats. Others are holding them until we can better understand our pharmaceutical urine's chemical effects passing into the water systems.

Happy tree frogs are singing tree frogs. They can be loud and very noticeable. Since a group of frogs is called a **chorus,** the tree frogs are indeed ***nature's singing chorus***.

REVIEW

1. What is the order name of most real tree frogs?

2. List three characteristics of tree frogs?

3. Explain what an amphibian is?

4. What is herpetology?

5. List three (of the five) characteristics of amphibians?

6. What is a *chorus*? What is the sub-title of this book?

7. What can we say about tree frogs' color, and why does this make identification more difficult?

8. How do tadpoles breathe?

9. Most tree frogs rarely drink water, so how do they hydrate?

10. What is one of the essential characteristics of identifying tree frogs?

TREE FROG

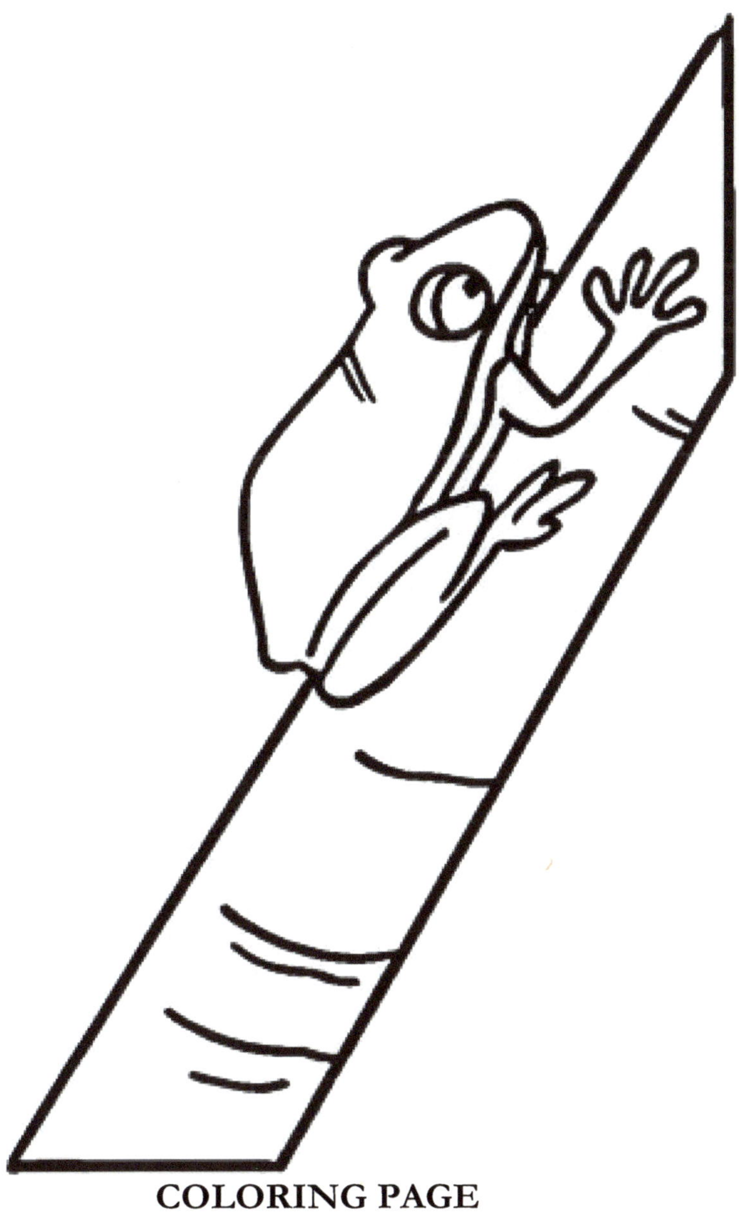

COLORING PAGE

Name:_____________________

Tree Frogs: Nature's Singing Chorus

Carefully read each statement or clue. Place the answers in the correct boxes. Use the Word Bank if necessary.

cannibalism   ectotherm   loudest   resonator   dimorphic   metamorphosis   tadpole

tongue   rainy   tympanum   clutches   spawn   amphibian   survival   herbivore

camouflage   nicitating

Across

1. Uses color to hide?
2. Third eye-lid? __________ membrane.
3. Living on land and living in water?
4. Vocal sac amplifies frog's croak like a __________
7. When sexes are different sizes; sexually __________
8. Name that causes the tadpole to turn into a frog?
12. Has gills, eats voraciously, and loses its tail?
13. Spit!
14. Spawn clusters or egg masses?
15. Frog's ear?

Down

1. Animal eats its own kind?
4. Breeding seasons tend to correspond with __________ season.
5. Term for term when frogs lay eggs?
6. Eats only plant material?
9. Has to obtain body heat from the environment?
10. Which male frogs are chosen to fertilize the females eggs?
11. Tadpole _______ rate is only about 8 out of 1000.

INTERESTING SOURCES TO CONSIDER

American Green Tree Frog!. Available at: https://youtu.be/d-lmJ4Kc7tc

Eastern Gray Treefrog or Cope's Gray Treefrog - Herp Quest #4. Available at: https://youtu.be/mGbXIod4R9M

Fabulous Frogs Nature Documentary. Available at: https://youtu.be/utlYuRhMmUs

Facts About Frogs & Toads: Secret Nature. Amphibian Documentary. Natural History Channel. Available at: https://youtu.be/RnxkJ-NFj38

Florida Frog Calls. Available at: https://www.floridamuseum.ufl.edu/science/florida-frog-calls/

Frogs Have A Secret Weapon To Catch Their Prey. Available at: https://youtu.be/dbcGzlmNIgE

Frogs National Geographic Documentary H.D. Available at: https://youtu.be/VGUkNtcB-jE

Frogs—Unexpected Desert Inhabitants. Available at: https://adventurepublications.net/2017/01/25/frogs/

Giant Screaming Frog! Available at: https://youtu.be/oS830cxjVFk

Gliding Leaf Frogs | Planet Earth | BBC Earth. Available at: https://youtu.be/tf1bytsDDho

Gray Tree Frog Mating Call. Available at: https://youtu.be/9bzotS1ow0Q

Gray tree frogs - Hundreds of them singing into the night! Available at: https://youtu.be/APyNDdvfXso

Gray Tree Frogs: Hundreds of them singing into the night. Available at: https://youtu.be/9bzotS1ow0Q

Green Tree frog calls. Available at: https://youtu.be/8fWjKQaPc0c

Green Treefrog Call Frogs of the Eastern U.S. Available at: https://youtu.be/UZcq-bMZAfA

Grey Tree Frog. Available from: https://nationalzoo.si.edu/animals/gray-tree-frog

Tree Frog Facts: Not Always in Trees. Animal Fact Files. Available at: https://youtu.be/9Zq4gD6MelM

ABOUT THE AUTHOR

Richard NeSmith is a native of Florida, USA. He grew up wading through the swamps of central Florida with his two younger brothers during the pre-Disney era, and unknowingly, falling in love with biology, wildlife, and nature. He has lived in seven American states, twice in Australia, and once in Mexico City. He holds eight university degrees and has taught for 14 years in secondary schools, here and abroad, and another 13 years as a professor in several American universities. His service includes professor of science education, Dean of Education, Campus Dean, as well as an online instructor. His passion for learning (and *how we learn*) did not develop until *after* graduating from high school. His only explanation for this is that *having a goal made all the difference in the world*. He enjoys reading, hiking, nature photography, golf, and tennis.

http://richardnesmith.obior.cc

Applied Principles of Education & Learning *presents*

APE-Learning

AMAZON AUTHOR's PAGE:

https://www.amazon.com/author/richardnesmith

Educational, wildlife, and naturalist books
Dr. Richard NeSmith.

Issue 1
Raccoons:
Friendly Bandits
Dr. Richard NeSmith

Issue 2
Sandhill Cranes
&
Pileated Woodpeckers
Flaming Redheads
Dr. Richard NeSmith

Issue 3
American
Alligators
&
Crocodiles
Dr. Richard NeSmith

Issue 4
Bobcats:
Ghostly Elusive
Dr. Richard NeSmith

Issue 5
Foxes:
Sneaky Rascals
Dr. Richard NeSmith

Issue 6
Armadillo:
Little Armored One
Dr. Richard NeSmith

Issue 7
Squirrels:
Bushy Tail Scampers
Dr. Richard NeSmith

Issue 8
River Otters:
Aquatic Clowns !
Dr. Richard NeSmith

Issue 9
Beavers:
Nature's Engineers !
Dr. Richard NeSmith

Issue 10
Black Bears
Titans of the Forest
Dr. Richard NeSmith

Issue 11
Freshwater
Turtles
Dr. Richard NeSmith

Issue 12
FUNGI, LICHENS
& MUSHROOMS
Dr. Richard NeSmith

Paperbacks: http://amazon.com/author/richardnesmith

e-books: https://bit.ly/3iuCgB3

---

[i] **Special thanks to the following who kindly provided permission to use their photographs.**

From Unsplash: David Clode, and Jean Louis-Aubert.

Also, special thanks to **DS Damm**, **Cindy Frasier**, **Tom Dotson**, **Greg Jowers,** and **Stacey Diamond** for their graciously sharing of some photographs of these beautiful creatures. Also, *special thanks to **Greg Jowers** for a beautiful photo making a picturesque book cover.*

Special thanks to Randy Johnson of Johnson ArtWorks, and his encouragement and assistance when I needed it most (http://johnsonartworks.com/)

JOHNSON ArtWorks

Thank you, everyone.

Love Learning —Love Nature—Love Living